Campbell's®

M'm! M'm!
HOMEMADE
IN MINUTES

pil
Publications
International Ltd.

Every recipe was developed and tested in the Campbell Soup Company Global Consumer Food Center by professional home economists.

"Campbell's," "Healthy Request," "Swanson," "Pace," "Prego," "V8" and "V8 Splash" are registered trademarks used with permission by Campbell Soup Company. "Pepperidge Farm" is a registered trademark used with permission by Pepperidge Farm, Incorporated.

Pictured on the front cover *(left to right):* Asian Chicken Stir-Fry *(page 6)* and Chicken Quesadillas *(page 7)*.

Pictured on the back cover *(clockwise from top left):* Chicken & Broccoli Alfredo *(page 4)*, Beef & Broccoli *(page 40)*, Easy Spaghetti & Meatballs *(page 42)* and Easy Chicken & Pasta *(page 12)*.

ISBN: 1-4127-2249-7

Manufactured in China.

8 7 6 5 4 3 2 1

Nutritional Analysis: Values are approximate; calculations are based upon food composition data in the Campbell Soup Company Master Data Base. Some variation in nutrition values may result from periodic product changes. Each analysis is based on the food items in the ingredient list, excluding optional ingredients and garnishes. When a choice is given for an ingredient, calculations are based upon the first choice listed.

Microwave Cooking: Microwave ovens vary in wattage. Use the cooking times as guidelines and check for doneness before adding more time.

Preparation/Cooking Times: Preparation times are based on the approximate amount of time required to assemble the recipe before cooking, baking or chilling. These times include preparation steps such as measuring, chopping and mixing. The fact that some preparations and cooking can be done simultaneously is taken into account. Preparation of optional ingredients and serving suggestions is not included.

M'm! M'm! HOMEMADE IN MINUTES

POULTRY IN NO TIME

Chicken & Broccoli Alfredo

Prep Time: 10 minutes   **Cook Time:** 15 minutes

- 6 ounces uncooked fettuccine
- 1 cup fresh or frozen broccoli flowerets
- 2 tablespoons butter or margarine
- 1 pound skinless, boneless chicken breasts, cubed
- 1 can (10¾ ounces) CAMPBELL'S® Condensed Cream of Mushroom Soup or 98% Fat Free Cream of Mushroom Soup
- ½ cup milk
- ½ cup grated Parmesan cheese
- ¼ teaspoon freshly ground pepper

1. Prepare fettuccine according to package directions. Add broccoli for last 4 minutes of cooking time. Drain.

2. In medium skillet over medium-high heat, heat butter. Add chicken and cook until browned, stirring often.

3. Add soup, milk, cheese, pepper and fettuccine mixture and cook through, stirring often.

Serves 4

Chicken & Broccoli Alfredo

Asian Chicken Stir-Fry

(photo on front cover)

Prep Time: 5 minutes   **Cook Time:** 20 minutes

1 tablespoon vegetable oil
1 pound skinless, boneless chicken breasts,
   cut into strips
1 can (10¾ ounces) CAMPBELL'S® Condensed
   Golden Mushroom Soup
3 tablespoons soy sauce
1 teaspoon garlic powder
1 bag (16 ounces) frozen vegetable combination,
   thawed
4 cups hot Broth Simmered Rice (page 40)

1. In medium skillet over medium-high heat, heat oil.
Add chicken and stir-fry until browned and juices evaporate.

2. Add soup, soy sauce and garlic powder. Heat to a boil.
Add vegetables and cook over medium heat until vegetables are
tender-crisp, stirring often. Serve over rice.   *Serves 4*

Asian Turkey Stir-Fry: Substitute 2 cups cubed cooked turkey for
chicken and oil. Omit step 1. In step 2 in medium skillet over
medium heat, heat soup, soy sauce and garlic powder to a boil.
Add turkey and vegetables and cook until vegetables are tender-
crisp, stirring often.

timesaver tip

To thaw vegetables, microwave on HIGH 4 minutes.

Chicken Quesadillas

(photo on front cover)

Prep Time: 5 minutes   **Cook Time:** 15 minutes

1 pound skinless, boneless chicken breasts, cubed
1 can (10¾ ounces) CAMPBELL'S® Condensed
   Cheddar Cheese Soup
½ cup PACE® Thick & Chunky Salsa or Picante Sauce
   (medium)
10 flour tortillas (8-inch)

1. Preheat oven to 425°F.

2. In medium nonstick skillet over medium-high heat, cook chicken 5 minutes or until no longer pink and juices evaporate, stirring often. Add soup and salsa. Heat through, stirring occasionally.

3. Place tortillas on 2 baking sheets. Top *half* of each tortilla with *about ⅓ cup* soup mixture. Spread to within ½ inch of edge. Moisten edges of tortilla with water. Fold over and seal edges together.

4. Bake 5 minutes or until hot.   *Serves 4*

Tip: Serve with Fiesta Rice (page 89).

timesaver tip

Substitute 2 cans (5 ounces *each*) SWANSON®
Premium Chunk Chicken Breast, drained, for fresh
chicken. In step 2 in medium saucepan mix soup,
salsa and chicken. Over medium heat, heat through,
stirring often. Proceed as in step 3.

Texas Two-Step Chicken Picante

Prep Time: 5 minutes   **Cook Time:** 20 minutes

4 skinless, boneless chicken breast halves
1½ cups PACE® Picante Sauce or
     Thick & Chunky Salsa
3 tablespoons packed light brown sugar
1 tablespoon Dijon-style mustard

1. Place chicken in 2-quart shallow baking dish.
Mix picante sauce, sugar and mustard. Pour over chicken.

2. Bake at 400°F. for 20 minutes or until chicken is no
longer pink.

Serves 4

Serve with hot cooked rice if desired.

Texas Two-Step Chicken Picante

15-Minute Chicken & Rice Dinner

Prep/Cook Time: 15 minutes

- 1 **tablespoon vegetable oil**
- 4 **skinless, boneless chicken breast halves (about 1 pound)**
- 1 **can (10¾ ounces) CAMPBELL'S® Condensed Cream of Chicken Soup or 98% Fat Free Cream of Chicken Soup**
- 1½ **cups water**
- ¼ **teaspoon paprika**
- ¼ **teaspoon pepper**
- 1½ **cups uncooked instant white rice**
- 2 **cups fresh or thawed frozen broccoli flowerets**

1. In medium skillet over medium-high heat, heat oil. Add chicken and cook 8 minutes or until browned. Set chicken aside. Pour off fat.

2. Add soup, water, paprika and pepper. Heat to a boil.

3. Stir in rice and broccoli. Place chicken on rice mixture. Reduce heat to low. Cover and cook 5 minutes or until chicken is no longer pink.

Serves 4

Chicken & Rice Dinner with Green Beans: Substitute 2 cups fresh *or* thawed frozen cut green beans for broccoli.

 **tip**

For creamier rice, increase water to 1⅔ cups.

15-Minute Chicken & Rice Dinner

Easy Chicken & Pasta

Prep Time: 5 minutes   **Cook Time:** 25 minutes

1   tablespoon vegetable oil
1   pound skinless, boneless chicken breasts, cut up
1   can (10¾ ounces) CAMPBELL'S® Condensed Cream of
      Mushroom Soup or 98% Fat Free Cream of
      Mushroom Soup
2¼ cups water
½   teaspoon dried basil leaves, crushed
2   cups frozen vegetable combination (broccoli,
      cauliflower, carrots)
2   cups *uncooked* corkscrew macaroni
      Grated Parmesan cheese

1. In medium skillet over medium-high heat, heat oil. Add chicken and cook until browned, stirring often. Set chicken aside.

2. Add soup, water, basil and vegetables. Heat to a boil. Add **uncooked** macaroni. Reduce heat to medium. Cook 10 minutes, stirring often.

3. Return chicken to pan. Cook 5 minutes more or until macaroni is done, stirring often. **Sprinkle with cheese.**   *Serves 4*

Your Choice Chicken & Pasta:

Choose a soup...	Choose a pasta...	Choose a combo...
CAMPBELL'S® Condensed Cream of Chicken Soup *or* 98% Fat Free Cream of Chicken Soup	Uncooked medium tube-shaped macaroni	Broccoli, corn and red peppers combination
CAMPBELL'S® Condensed Cheddar Cheese Soup	Uncooked spaghetti, broken in half*	Stir-fry *or* Oriental vegetables, no sauce added
CAMPBELL'S® Condensed Cream of Celery Soup *or* 98% Fat Free Cream of Celery Soup	Uncooked bow tie pasta	Peas and carrots

Increase water to 2½ cups. 8 ounces uncooked spaghetti = 2 cups.

Easy Chicken & Pasta

Quick Chicken Parmigiana

Prep Time: 5 minutes   **Cook Time:** 15 minutes

- 1 package (about 10 ounces) frozen fully cooked breaded chicken patties or 1 package (about 14 ounces) refrigerated fully cooked breaded chicken cutlets
- 1 jar (28 ounces) PREGO® Traditional Pasta Sauce
- 2 tablespoons grated Parmesan cheese
- ½ cup shredded mozzarella cheese (2 ounces)
- 4 cups hot cooked spaghetti (about 8 ounces uncooked)

1. In 2-quart shallow baking dish arrange patties. Top each with ¼ **cup** pasta sauce. Sprinkle with Parmesan cheese and mozzarella cheese.

2. Bake at 400°F. for 15 minutes or until chicken is hot and cheese is melted.

3. Heat remaining sauce until hot. Serve sauce with chicken and spaghetti.

Serves 4

Time Saver: In 2-quart shallow microwave-safe baking dish arrange patties. Microwave on HIGH 4 minutes (3 minutes for refrigerated cutlets). Top each patty with ¼ **cup** pasta sauce, **1 teaspoon** Parmesan cheese and **2 tablespoons** mozzarella cheese. Microwave 2 minutes more or until sauce is hot and cheese is melted.

Chicken Nuggets Parmigiana: Substitute 1 package (10 to 13 ounces) frozen **or** refrigerated fully cooked breaded chicken nuggets for chicken patties. In 2-quart shallow microwave-safe baking dish arrange nuggets. Microwave on HIGH 3½ minutes (2½ minutes for refrigerated). Pour pasta sauce evenly over nuggets. Top with cheeses. Microwave 2 minutes more or until sauce is hot and cheese is melted.

Top to bottom: Mushroom Mozzarella Bruschetta (page 71) and Quick Chicken Parmigiana

Skillet Herb Roasted Chicken

Prep Time: 10 minutes   **Cook Time:** 20 minutes

4 skinless, boneless chicken breast halves (about 1 pound)
¼ teaspoon ground sage
¼ teaspoon dried thyme leaves, crushed
   Vegetable cooking spray
2 cloves garlic, minced
1 can (10¾ ounces) CAMPBELL'S® HEALTHY REQUEST Condensed Cream of Chicken Soup
½ cup water
4 cups hot cooked rice, cooked without salt

1. Sprinkle chicken with sage and thyme.

2. Spray medium nonstick skillet with cooking spray and heat over medium heat 1 minute. Add chicken and cook 15 minutes or until chicken is browned and no longer pink. Remove and keep warm.

3. Remove pan from heat. Spray with cooking spray. Add garlic and cook 30 seconds or until lightly browned.

4. Add soup and water. Reduce heat to low and heat through. Serve over chicken with rice. *Serves 4*

Nutritional Values per Serving: Calories 457, Total Fat 5g, Saturated Fat 2g, Cholesterol 79mg, Sodium 361mg, Total Carbohydrate 65g, Protein 33g

Skillet Herb Roasted Chicken

Country Mustard Chicken

Prep Time: 5 minutes   **Cook Time:** 20 minutes

Vegetable cooking spray
4 skinless, boneless chicken breast halves
1 jar (12 ounces) CAMPBELL'S® Slow Roast
Chicken Gravy
1 tablespoon country-style Dijon mustard
½ teaspoon garlic powder

1. Spray medium skillet with cooking spray and heat over medium-high heat 1 minute. Add chicken and cook 10 minutes or until browned. Set chicken aside.

2. Add gravy, mustard and garlic powder. Heat to a boil. Return chicken to pan. Reduce heat to low. Cover and cook 5 minutes or until chicken is no longer pink. Serve with noodles if desired. Sprinkle with chopped parsley.   *Serves 4*

QUICK SIDE DISH Broccoli & Noodles Supreme

Prep Time: 5 minutes   **Cook Time:** 20 minutes

3 cups uncooked medium egg noodles
2 cups fresh or frozen broccoli flowerets
1 can (10¾ ounces) CAMPBELL'S® Condensed
Cream of Chicken Soup or 98% Fat Free Cream
of Chicken Soup
½ cup sour cream
⅓ cup grated Parmesan cheese
⅛ teaspoon pepper

In large saucepan prepare noodles according to package directions. Add broccoli for last 5 minutes of cooking time. Drain. In same pan mix soup, sour cream, cheese, pepper and noodle mixture. Over medium heat, heat through, stirring occasionally.   *Serves 5*

*Left to right: Broccoli & Noodles Supreme
and Country Mustard Chicken*

Tomato-Basil Chicken

Prep Time: 5 minutes   **Cook Time:** 20 minutes

- 1 tablespoon vegetable oil
- 4 skinless, boneless breast halves (about 1 pound)
- 1 can (10¾ ounces) CAMPBELL'S® Condensed Tomato Soup
- ½ cup milk
- 2 tablespoons grated Parmesan cheese
- ½ teaspoon dried basil leaves, crushed
- ¼ teaspoon garlic powder or 2 cloves garlic, minced
- 4 cups hot cooked medium tube-shaped macaroni (about 3 cups uncooked)

1. In medium skillet over medium-high heat, heat oil. Add chicken and cook 10 minutes or until browned. Set chicken aside. Pour off fat.

2. Add soup, milk, cheese, basil and garlic powder. Heat to a boil. Return chicken to pan. Reduce heat to low. Cover and cook 5 minutes or until chicken is no longer pink. Serve with macaroni.

Serves 4

tip

Cook pasta as chicken is browning. For extra flavor, simmer pasta in broth (see Simple Seasoned Pasta, page 28).

Top to Bottom: Honey-Mustard Chicken (page 31) and Tomato-Basil Chicken

Crunchy No-Fry Chicken

Prep Time: 10 minutes   **Cook Time:** 20 minutes

¾ **cup finely crushed corn flakes**
½ **teaspoon garlic powder**
⅛ **teaspoon black pepper**
⅛ **teaspoon ground red pepper**
4 **skinless, boneless chicken breast halves**
¼ **cup SWANSON® Chicken Broth**

1. Mix corn flakes, garlic powder, black pepper and red pepper.
Dip chicken into broth. Coat with corn flake mixture.

2. Place chicken on baking sheet. Bake at 400°F. for 20 minutes or
until chicken is no longer pink.   *Serves 4*

QUICK SIDE DISH Glazed Snow Peas & Carrots

Prep Time: 15 minutes   **Cook Time:** 10 minutes

4 **teaspoons cornstarch**
1 **can (14½ ounces) SWANSON® Vegetable Broth**
4 **medium carrots, sliced (about 2 cups)**
1 **medium onion, chopped (about ½ cup)**
¾ **pound snow peas (about 4 cups)**
1 **teaspoon lemon juice**

1. In cup mix cornstarch and *1 cup* broth until smooth. Set aside.

2. In medium skillet over high heat, heat remaining broth to a boil.
Add carrots and onion. Reduce heat to medium. Cover and
cook 5 minutes or until carrots are tender-crisp. Add snow peas.
Cook 2 minutes.

3. Stir cornstarch mixture and add. Cook until mixture boils and
thickens, stirring constantly. Stir in lemon juice.   *Serves 8*

*Left to right: Crunchy No-Fry Chicken, Glazed
Snow Peas & Carrots and Garlic Mashed Potatoes (page 87)*

Lemon Broccoli Chicken

Prep Time: 5 minutes   **Cook Time:** 20 minutes

- 1 **lemon**
- 1 **tablespoon vegetable oil**
- 4 **skinless, boneless chicken breast halves (about 1 pound)**
- 1 **can (10¾ ounces) CAMPBELL'S® Condensed Cream of Broccoli Soup or 98% Fat Free Cream of Broccoli Soup**
- ¼ **cup milk**
- ⅛ **teaspoon pepper**

1. Cut 4 thin slices of lemon and set aside. Squeeze 2 teaspoons juice from remaining lemon and set aside.

2. In medium skillet over medium-high heat, heat oil. Add chicken and cook 10 minutes or until browned. Set chicken aside. Pour off fat.

3. Add soup, milk, reserved lemon juice and pepper. Heat to a boil. Return chicken to pan. Top with lemon slices. Reduce heat to low. Cover and cook 5 minutes or until chicken is no longer pink.

Serves 8

tip

Looking for a quick and delicious side dish your family will love? Top your favorite cooked pasta shape with PREGO® Pasta Sauce, a perfect accompaniment to chicken, pork or meat loaf!

Lemon Broccoli Chicken

25-Minute Chicken & Noodles

Prep Time: 10 minutes   **Cook Time:** 15 minutes

- **1 can (14½ ounces) SWANSON® Chicken Broth (1¾ cups)**
- **½ teaspoon dried basil leaves, crushed**
- **⅛ teaspoon pepper**
- **2 cups frozen vegetable combination (broccoli, cauliflower, carrots)**
- **2 cups uncooked medium egg noodles**
- **2 cups cubed cooked chicken**

1. In medium skillet mix broth, basil, pepper and vegetables. Over medium-high heat, heat to a boil. Reduce heat to medium. Cover and cook 5 minutes.

2. Stir in noodles. Cover and cook 5 minutes, stirring often. Add chicken and heat through.

Serves 4

tip

For 2 cups cubed cooked chicken: In medium saucepan over medium heat, in 4 cups boiling water, cook 1 pound skinless, boneless chicken breasts **or** thighs, cubed, 5 minutes or until chicken is no longer pink. Chicken should be cooked to a minimum internal temperature of 165°F.

25-Minute Chicken & Noodles

Chicken Mozzarella

Prep Time: 10 minutes   **Cook Time:** 20 minutes

> 4 skinless, boneless chicken breast halves (about 1 pound)
> 1 can (10¾ ounces) CAMPBELL'S® HEALTHY REQUEST Condensed Tomato Soup
> ½ teaspoon Italian seasoning or dried oregano leaves, crushed
> ½ teaspoon garlic powder
> ¼ cup shredded mozzarella cheese (1 ounce)
> 4 cups hot cooked corkscrew macaroni (about 3 cups uncooked), cooked without salt

1. Place chicken in 2-quart shallow baking dish. Mix soup, Italian seasoning and garlic powder. Spoon over chicken and bake at 400°F. for 20 minutes or until chicken is no longer pink.

2. Sprinkle cheese over chicken. Remove chicken. Stir sauce. Serve with macaroni.

Serves 4

Nutritional Values per Serving: Calories 559, Total Fat 7g, Saturated Fat 2g, Cholesterol 78mg, Sodium 385mg, Total Carbohydrate 80g, Protein 41g

QUICK SIDE DISH **Simple Seasoned Pasta**

Prep Time: 5 minutes   **Cook Time:** 15 minutes

> 1 can (14½ ounces) SWANSON® Seasoned Chicken Broth with Italian Herbs
> 1½ cups uncooked corkscrew macaroni

In medium saucepan over medium-high heat, heat broth to a boil. Stir in macaroni. **Reduce heat to medium.** Simmer gently 10 minutes or until macaroni is done, stirring occasionally.   *Serves 2*

Chicken Mozzarella and Simple Seasoned Pasta

Southwest Salsa Chicken with Fresh Greens

Prep Time: 10 minutes   **Cook Time:** 10 minutes

1 tablespoon chili powder
1 teaspoon ground cumin
6 skinless, boneless chicken breast halves (about 1½ pounds), cut into 3x1-inch strips
1 tablespoon olive oil
1 cup PACE® Chunky Salsa
¼ cup water
1 bag (about 7 ounces) mixed salad greens (6 cups)

1. Mix chili powder and cumin. Add chicken and toss to coat.

2. Heat a heavy skillet on high heat. Add oil and chicken. Cook until chicken is blackened and no longer pink, stirring often. Remove chicken.

3. Add salsa and water and heat through. Divide greens among 6 plates. Top each with chicken and salsa.   *Serves 6*

Honey-Mustard Chicken

(photo on page 21)

Prep Time: 10 minutes   **Cook Time:** 20 minutes

- 1 tablespoon butter or margarine
- 4 skinless, boneless chicken breast halves
- 1 can (10¾ ounces) CAMPBELL'S® Condensed Cream of Chicken Soup or 98% Fat Free Cream of Chicken Soup
- ¼ cup mayonnaise
- 2 tablespoons honey
- 1 tablespoon spicy brown mustard
- Chopped toasted pecans or walnuts

1. In medium skillet over medium-high heat, heat butter. Add chicken and cook 10 minutes or until browned. Set chicken aside.

2. Add soup, mayonnaise, honey and mustard. Heat to a boil. Return chicken to pan. Reduce heat to low. Cover and cook 5 minutes or until chicken is no longer pink. Sprinkle with pecans.   *Serves 4*

 **tip**

Serve with rice if desired.

Chicken Dijon

Prep Time: 5 minutes   **Cook Time:** 20 minutes

Vegetable cooking spray
4 skinless, boneless chicken breast halves (about 1 pound)
1 can (10¾ ounces) CAMPBELL'S® Condensed Cream of Celery Soup or 98% Fat Free Cream of Celery Soup
⅔ cup water
1 tablespoon Dijon-style mustard
⅛ teaspoon pepper
4 cups hot cooked rice

1. Spray medium skillet with cooking spray and heat over medium-high heat 1 minute. Add chicken and cook 10 minutes or until browned. Set chicken aside.

2. Add soup, water, mustard and pepper. Heat to a boil. Return chicken to pan. Reduce heat to low. Cover and cook 5 minutes or until chicken is no longer pink. Serve with rice.   *Serves 4*

tip

The versatile Vegetable Stir-Fry (page 61),
pictured right as a side dish, also works as a main
dish served over rice.

Left to right: Vegetable Stir-Fry (page 61)
and Chicken Dijon

Santa Fe Chicken

Prep Time: 10 minutes   **Cook Time:** 20 minutes

- 1 tablespoon all-purpose flour
- 1 tablespoon chili powder
- 4 skinless, boneless chicken breast halves (about 1 pound)
- 2 tablespoons vegetable oil
- 1 can (10¾ ounces) CAMPBELL'S® Condensed Tomato Soup
- ¼ cup shredded Cheddar or Monterey Jack cheese (1 ounce)

1. Mix flour and chili powder. Coat chicken with flour mixture.

2. In medium skillet over medium heat, heat oil. Add chicken and cook 10 minutes or until browned. Set chicken aside. Pour off fat.

3. Add soup. Heat to a boil. Return chicken to pan. Reduce heat to low. Cover and cook 5 minutes or until chicken is no longer pink. Sprinkle with cheese.   *Serves 4*

QUICK SIDE DISH Simple Two-Step Nacho Pasta

Prep Time: 5 minutes   **Cook Time:** 20 minutes

- 4 cups uncooked corkscrew macaroni
- 1 can (11 ounces) CAMPBELL'S® Condensed Fiesta Nacho Cheese Soup
- ½ cup milk

1. In large saucepan prepare macaroni according to package directions. Drain.

2. In same pan mix soup, milk and macaroni. Over medium heat, heat through, stirring often.   *Serves 4*

Left to right: Simple Two-Step Nacho Pasta and Santa Fe Chicken

Crispy Chicken with Asparagus Sauce

Prep Time: 10 minutes   **Cook Time:** 20 minutes

4 skinless, boneless chicken breast halves or
   8 skinless, boneless chicken thighs
   (about 1 pound)
1 egg or 2 egg whites, beaten
½ cup dry bread crumbs
2 tablespoons vegetable oil
1 can (10¾ ounces) CAMPBELL'S® Condensed
   Cream of Asparagus Soup
⅓ cup milk
⅓ cup water
   Grated Parmesan cheese

1. Dip chicken into egg. Coat with bread crumbs.

2. In medium skillet over medium heat, heat oil. Add chicken and cook 15 minutes or until chicken is browned and no longer pink. Remove and keep warm. Pour off fat.

3. Add soup, milk and water. Reduce heat to low and heat through. Serve over chicken. Sprinkle with cheese. Serve with rice if desired.

Serves 4

tip

Try this dish over Broth Simmered Rice (page 40),
with vegetables steamed in broth.

Crispy Chicken with Asparagus Sauce and
Quick Lemon-Broccoli Rice (page 89)

MEAT DISHES IN MINUTES

Shortcut Beef Stew

Prep Time: 5 minutes   **Cook Time:** 25 minutes

1 tablespoon vegetable oil
1 pound boneless beef sirloin steak, cut into
    1-inch cubes
1 can (10¾ ounces) CAMPBELL'S® Condensed
    Tomato Soup
1 can (10¾ ounces) CAMPBELL'S® Condensed
    French Onion Soup
1 tablespoon Worcestershire sauce
1 bag (24 ounces) frozen vegetables for stew
    (potatoes, carrots, celery)

1. In Dutch oven over medium-high heat, heat oil. Add beef and cook until browned, stirring often. Set beef aside.

2. Add soups, Worcestershire and vegetables. Heat to a boil. Return beef to pan. Reduce heat to low. Cover and cook 10 minutes or until vegetables are tender, stirring occasionally.

Serves 4

Shortcut Beef Stew

Beef & Broccoli

Prep Time: 10 minutes   **Cook Time:** 20 minutes

1 pound boneless beef sirloin or top round steak,
¾-inch thick
1 tablespoon vegetable oil
1 can (10¾ ounces) CAMPBELL'S® Condensed
Tomato Soup
3 tablespoons soy sauce
1 tablespoon vinegar
1 teaspoon garlic powder
¼ teaspoon red pepper flakes (optional)
3 cups fresh or thawed frozen broccoli flowerets

1. Slice beef into very thin strips.

2. In medium skillet over medium-high heat, heat oil. Add beef and stir-fry until browned and juices evaporate.

3. Add soup, soy sauce, vinegar, garlic powder and pepper flakes. Heat to a boil. Add broccoli and cook over medium heat until broccoli is tender-crisp, stirring often. Serve with Broth Simmered Rice.

Serves 4

QUICK SIDE DISH **Broth Simmered Rice**

Prep/Cook Time: 10 minutes   **Stand Time:** 5 minutes

1 can (10½ ounces) CAMPBELL'S® Condensed
Chicken Broth
¾ cup water
2 cups uncooked instant rice

In medium saucepan over medium-high heat, heat broth and water to a boil. Stir in rice. Cover and remove from heat. Let stand 5 minutes. Fluff with fork.

Serves 4

Left to right: Beef & Broccoli and Broth Simmered Rice

Easy Spaghetti & Meatballs

Prep Time: 15 minutes   **Cook Time:** 10 minutes

1 pound ground beef
2 tablespoons water
⅓ cup seasoned dry bread crumbs
1 egg, beaten
1 jar (28 ounces) PREGO® Traditional Pasta Sauce or
    Pasta Sauce Flavored with Meat
4 cups hot cooked spaghetti

1. Mix beef, water, bread crumbs and egg. Shape meat mixture into 12 (2-inch) meatballs. Arrange in 2-quart shallow microwave-safe baking dish.

2. Microwave on HIGH 5 minutes or until meatballs are no longer pink (160°F.). Pour off fat. Pour pasta sauce over meatballs. Cover and microwave 3 minutes more or until sauce is hot. Serve over spaghetti.

Serves 4

Zesty Ziti

Prep Time: 10 minutes   **Cook Time:** 20 minutes

1 pound Italian sausage, cut into ½-inch pieces
1 large onion, chopped (about 1 cup)
1 medium green pepper, diced (about 1 cup)
1 jar (28 ounces) PREGO® Three Cheese Pasta Sauce
4½ cups hot cooked medium tube-shaped macaroni

1. In medium skillet over medium heat, cook sausage, onion and pepper until sausage is no longer pink. Pour off fat.

2. Add pasta sauce. Heat to a boil. Serve over macaroni. Top with grated Parmesan cheese.

Serves 4

*Top to bottom: Zesty Ziti
and Easy Spaghetti & Meatballs*

Fiesta Taco Salad

Prep Time: 10 minutes   **Cook Time:** 15 minutes

1 **pound ground beef**
2 **tablespoons chili powder**
1 **can (10¾ ounces) CAMPBELL'S® Condensed Tomato Soup**
8 **cups salad greens torn into bite-size pieces**
2 **cups tortilla chips**
   Chopped tomato
   Sliced green onions
   Shredded Cheddar cheese
   Sliced pitted ripe olives

1. In medium skillet over medium-high heat, cook beef and chili powder until beef is browned, stirring to separate meat. Pour off fat.

2. Add soup. Reduce heat to low and heat through.

3. Arrange salad greens and chips on platter. Spoon meat mixture over salad greens. Top with tomato, onions, cheese and olives.

Serves 4

timesaver tip

Save time by using packaged pre-shredded Cheddar cheese and checking the salad bar at your supermarket for pre-cut greens, toppers and trimmings.

Fiesta Taco Salad

Two-Bean Chili

Prep Time: 10 minutes   **Cook Time:** 15 minutes

1 pound ground beef
1 large green pepper, chopped (about 1 cup)
1 large onion, chopped (about 1 cup)
2 tablespoons chili powder
¼ teaspoon black pepper
3 cups CAMPBELL'S® Tomato Juice
1 can (about 15 ounces) kidney beans, rinsed and
    drained
1 can (about 15 ounces) great Northern or white
    kidney (cannellini) beans, rinsed and drained
    Sour cream
    Sliced green onions
    Shredded Cheddar cheese
    Chopped tomato

1. In medium skillet over medium-high heat, cook beef, green pepper, onion, chili powder and black pepper until beef is browned, stirring to separate meat. Pour off fat.

2. Add tomato juice and beans and heat through. Top with sour cream, green onions, cheese and tomato.   *Serves 6*

tip

For a cool refresher, mix ¾ cup CAMPBELL'S®
Tomato Juice with ¼ cup ginger ale and
1 tablespoon lemon juice. Serve over ice and
garnish with lemon slice.

*Top to bottom: Hearty Vegetarian Chili (page 60)
and Two-Bean Chili*

Spicy Salsa Mac & Beef

Prep Time: 5 minutes   **Cook Time:** 25 minutes

1 **pound ground beef**
1 **can (10½ ounces) CAMPBELL'S® Condensed Beef Broth**
1⅓ **cups water**
2 **cups uncooked medium shell or elbow macaroni**
1 **can (10¾ ounces) CAMPBELL'S® Condensed Cheddar Cheese Soup**
1 **cup PACE® Thick & Chunky Salsa**

1. In medium skillet over medium-high heat, cook beef until browned, stirring to separate meat. Pour off fat.

2. Add broth and water. Heat to a boil. Stir in macaroni. Reduce heat to medium. Cook 10 minutes or until macaroni is done, stirring often.

3. Stir in soup and salsa and heat through.   *Serves 4*

tip

Pair this dynamic kid-pleasing dish with a glass of V8 SPLASH®. The light taste of tropical fruit juices makes a great go-with and delivers 100% of Vitamins A and C.

Spicy Salsa Mac & Beef

Quick Pepper Steak

Prep Time: 10 minutes   **Cook Time:** 20 minutes

- 1 **pound boneless beef sirloin or top round steak, ¾-inch thick**
- 2 **tablespoons vegetable oil**
- 2 **medium green or red peppers, cut into 2-inch-long strips (about 3 cups)**
- 1 **medium onion, cut into wedges**
- ½ **teaspoon garlic powder**
- 1 **can (10¼ ounces) CAMPBELL'S® Beef Gravy**
- 1 **tablespoon Worcestershire sauce**
- 4 **cups hot cooked rice**

1. Slice beef into thin strips.

2. In medium skillet over medium-high heat, heat *half* the oil. Add beef in 2 batches and stir-fry until browned. Set beef aside.

3. Reduce heat to medium. Add remaining oil. Add peppers, onion and garlic powder and stir-fry until tender-crisp. Pour off fat.

4. Add gravy and Worcestershire. Heat to a boil. Return beef to pan. Reduce heat to low and heat through. Serve over rice.

Serves 4

tip

Instead of choosing either green or red peppers,
try both to vary the flavor and create
a colorful dish!

Quick Pepper Steak

Picante Beef & Beans

Prep Time: 10 minutes   **Cook Time:** 20 minutes

2   tablespoons cornstarch
2   tablespoons water
1   tablespoon vegetable oil
1   pound boneless beef sirloin steak, cut into 1-inch cubes
1   tablespoon chili powder
¾   cup PACE® Picante Sauce or Thick & Chunky Salsa
1   can (about 16 ounces) black beans, undrained
1   can (about 15 ounces) pinto beans, undrained
1   can (about 14½ ounces) stewed tomatoes

1. In cup mix cornstarch and water until smooth. Set aside.

2. In Dutch oven over medium-high heat, heat oil. Add beef and chili powder and cook until beef is browned, stirring often.

3. Add picante sauce, beans and tomatoes. Heat to a boil. Reduce heat to low. Cover and cook 5 minutes or until beef is done.

4. Stir cornstarch mixture and add. Cook until mixture boils and thickens, stirring constantly.   *Serves 6*

tip

PACE® Picante Sauce and Thick & Chunky Salsa are available in mild, medium and hot varieties. Try the one your family likes best.

Picante Beef & Beans

Steak & Mushroom Florentine

Prep Time: 10 minutes   **Cook Time:** 10 minutes

1   pound boneless beef sirloin or top round steak, ¾-inch thick
2   tablespoons vegetable oil
1   small onion, sliced (about ¼ cup)
4   cups baby spinach leaves, washed
1   can (10¾ ounces) CAMPBELL'S® Condensed Cream of Mushroom Soup or 98% Fat Free Cream of Mushroom Soup
1   cup water
1   large tomato, thickly sliced
    Freshly ground black pepper

1. Slice beef into very thin strips.

2. Heat *1 tablespoon* oil in medium nonstick skillet over medium-high heat. Add beef and cook until browned. Set beef aside.

3. Heat remaining oil over medium heat. Add onion and cook until tender-crisp. Add spinach and cook just until spinach is wilted.

4. Add soup and water. Heat to a boil. Return beef to skillet and heat through. Serve beef mixture over tomato. Season to taste with black pepper.   *Serves 4*

Steak & Mushroom Florentine

Roast Pork with Citrus Molasses au Jus

Prep Time: 10 minutes   **Cook Time:** 20 minutes
Stand Time: 10 minutes

1 pound whole pork tenderloin
2 teaspoons vegetable oil
½ teaspoon dried rosemary or thyme leaves, crushed
Ground black pepper (optional)
1 tablespoon cornstarch
1½ cups SWANSON® Chicken or Natural Goodness™ Chicken Broth
2 tablespoons orange juice
2 tablespoons molasses
1 tablespoon packed brown sugar
¼ cup chopped shallots or onion
2 medium oranges, peeled and cut into sections

1. Preheat oven to 425°F. Brush pork with **1 teaspoon** oil. Sprinkle with rosemary and black pepper, if desired. Place in roasting pan.

2. Roast for 20 minutes or until temperature reads 155°F. on meat thermometer. Remove pork from pan and let stand 10 minutes.

3. Mix cornstarch, broth, orange juice, molasses and brown sugar until smooth. Set aside.

4. Heat remaining oil in medium saucepan over medium heat. Add shallots and cook until tender. Stir cornstarch mixture and add. Cook until mixture boils and thickens, stirring constantly. Stir in oranges and heat through. Serve with pork.   *Serves 4*

Roast Pork with Citrus Molasses au Jus

EASY FISH & MEATLESS

Garlic Shrimp & Pasta

Prep Time: 15 minutes   **Cook Time:** 10 minutes

- 1 can (14½ ounces) SWANSON® Chicken Broth (1¾ cups)
- 2 cloves garlic, minced
- 3 tablespoons chopped fresh parsley or 1 tablespoon dried parsley flakes
- 2 tablespoons cornstarch
- 2 tablespoons lemon juice
- ⅛ teaspoon ground red pepper
- 1 pound medium shrimp, shelled and deveined
- 4 cups hot cooked thin spaghetti (about 8 ounces uncooked)

1. In medium saucepan mix broth, garlic, parsley, cornstarch, lemon juice and pepper. Over medium-high heat, heat to a boil. Cook until mixture thickens, stirring constantly.

2. Add shrimp. Cook 5 minutes more or until shrimp turn pink, stirring often. Toss with spaghetti.   *Serves 4*

Top to bottom: Quick 'n' Easy Salmon (page 60), Vegetable Rice Pilaf (page 88) and Garlic Shrimp & Pasta

Quick 'n' Easy Salmon

(photo on page 59)

Prep Time: 5 minutes   **Cook Time:** 15 minutes

1 can (14½ ounces) SWANSON® Chicken Broth (1¾ cups)
¼ cup Chablis or other dry white wine
¼ teaspoon dried dill weed, crushed
4 thin lemon slices
4 salmon steaks, 1-inch thick (about 1½ pounds)

1. In medium skillet mix broth, wine, dill and lemon. Over medium-high heat, heat to a boil.

2. Place fish in broth mixture. Reduce heat to low. Cover and cook 10 minutes or until fish flakes easily when tested with a fork. Discard poaching liquid.   *Serves 4*

Hearty Vegetarian Chili

(photo on page 47)

Prep Time: 10 minutes   **Cook Time:** 20 minutes

2 tablespoons vegetable oil
1 large onion, chopped (about 1 cup)
1 small green pepper, chopped (about ½ cup)
¼ teaspoon garlic powder or 2 cloves garlic, minced
1 tablespoon chili powder
½ teaspoon ground cumin
2½ cups V8® 100% Vegetable Juice
1 can (16 ounces) black beans, rinsed and drained
1 can (15 ounces) pinto beans, rinsed and drained

1. In large saucepan over medium heat, heat oil. Add onion, pepper, garlic powder, chili powder and cumin and cook until tender.

2. Add vegetable juice. Heat to a boil. Reduce heat to low. Cook 5 minutes. Add beans and heat through.   *Serves 4*

Vegetable Stir-Fry

(photo on page 33)

Prep Time: 15 minutes   **Cook Time:** 10 minutes

- 1   can (14½ ounces) SWANSON® Vegetable Broth
- 2   tablespoons cornstarch
- 1   tablespoon soy sauce
- ¼   teaspoon ground ginger
- 1   tablespoon vegetable oil
- 5   cups cut-up vegetables*
- ⅛   teaspoon garlic powder or 1 clove garlic, minced

1. In bowl mix broth, cornstarch, soy sauce and ginger until smooth. Set aside.

2. In medium skillet over medium-high heat, heat oil. Add vegetables and garlic powder and stir-fry until tender-crisp.

3. Stir cornstarch mixture and add. Cook until mixture boils and thickens, stirring constantly.

Serves 4 as a main dish or 8 as a side dish

Use a combination of broccoli flowerets, sliced mushrooms, sliced carrots, sliced celery, red or green pepper strips and sliced green onions.

Tomato Mac 'n' Cheese

Prep/Cook Time: 20 minutes

- 1   can CAMPBELL'S® Cheddar Cheese Soup
- 1   cup PREGO® Traditional Pasta Sauce
- ⅓   cup milk
- 4   cups cooked elbow pasta
-      Grated Parmesan cheese

1. Mix soup, pasta sauce, milk and pasta in saucepan. Heat through.

2. Serve with cheese.

Serves 5

Cajun Fish

Prep Time: 10 minutes   **Cook Time:** 15 minutes

1   tablespoon vegetable oil
1   small green pepper, diced (about ⅔ cup)
½   teaspoon dried oregano leaves, crushed
1   can (10¾ ounces) CAMPBELL'S® Condensed
        Tomato Soup
⅓   cup water
⅛   teaspoon garlic powder
⅛   teaspoon black pepper
⅛   teaspoon ground red pepper
1   pound firm white fish fillets (cod, haddock or halibut)

1. In medium skillet over medium heat, heat oil. Add green pepper and oregano and cook until tender-crisp, stirring often. Add soup, water, garlic powder, black pepper and red pepper. Heat to a boil.

2. Place fish in soup mixture. Reduce heat to low. Cover and cook 5 minutes or until fish flakes easily when tested with a fork. Serve with rice if desired.

Serves 4

QUICK SIDE DISH Slim & Savory Vegetables

Prep Time: 15 minutes   **Cook Time:** 10 minutes

1   can (14½ ounces) SWANSON® Chicken Broth
        (1¾ cups)
4   cups cut-up vegetables*

In medium saucepan mix broth and vegetables. Over medium-high heat, heat to a boil. Reduce heat to low. Cover and cook 5 minutes or until vegetables are tender-crisp. Drain.

Serves 6

*Use a combination of broccoli flowerets, cauliflower flowerets, sliced carrot and sliced celery.

Left to right: Cajun Fish and Slim & Savory Vegetables

Primavera Fish Fillets

Prep Time: 10 minutes   **Cook Time:** 20 minutes

- 1 **large carrot, cut into matchstick-thin strips (about 1 cup)**
- 2 **stalks celery, cut into matchstick-thin strips (about 1 cup)**
- 1 **small onion, diced (about ¼ cup)**
- ¼ **cup water**
- 2 **tablespoons Chablis or other dry white wine**
- ½ **teaspoon dried thyme leaves, crushed**
  Generous dash pepper
- 1 **can (10¾ ounces) CAMPBELL'S® HEALTHY REQUEST Condensed Cream of Mushroom Soup**
- 1 **pound firm white fish fillets (cod, haddock or halibut)**

1. In medium skillet mix carrot, celery, onion, water, wine, thyme and pepper. Over medium-high heat, heat to a boil. Reduce heat to low. Cover and cook 5 minutes or until vegetables are tender-crisp.

2. Stir in soup. Over medium heat, heat to a boil.

3. Place fish in soup mixture. Reduce heat to low. Cover and cook 5 minutes or until fish flakes easily when tested with a fork.

Serves 4

Nutritional Values per Serving: Calories 160, Total Fat 2g, Saturated Fat 1g, Cholesterol 52mg, Sodium 379mg, Total Carbohydrate 11g, Protein 21g

In this recipe, CAMPBELL'S® HEALTHY REQUEST creates a lower fat alternative to a traditional Newburg-style sauce made with butter and cream.

Primavera Fish Fillet

Seafood & Mushroom Shells

Bake Time: 30 minutes*   **Prep/Cook Time:** 20 minutes

- 1 package (10 ounces) PEPPERIDGE FARM® Frozen Puff Pastry Shells
- 4 tablespoons unsalted butter
- 2½ cups thinly sliced mushrooms (about 8 ounces)
- 1 can (10¾ ounces) CAMPBELL'S® Condensed Cream of Mushroom Soup or 98% Fat Free Cream of Mushroom Soup
- ½ cup dry white wine or vermouth
- 1 tablespoon lemon juice
- 1 pound firm white fish (cod, haddock or halibut), cut into 1-inch pieces
- ½ cup grated Parmesan cheese

1. Bake pastry shells according to package directions.

2. In medium skillet over medium heat, heat butter. Add mushrooms and cook until tender.

3. Add soup, wine, lemon juice and fish. Cook 5 minutes or until fish flakes easily when tested with a fork.

4. Serve in pastry shells. Sprinkle with cheese.   *Serves 4*

Bake pastry shells while preparing fish mixture.

Top to bottom: Seafood & Mushroom Shells and Creamy Vegetables in Pastry Shells (page 91)

SPEEDY SNACKS & MINI-MEALS

Chicken Noodle Soup Express

Prep Time: 10 minutes   **Cook Time:** 15 minutes

2 cans (14½ ounces each) SWANSON® Chicken
   Broth (3½ cups)
   Generous dash pepper
1 medium carrot, sliced (about ½ cup)
1 stalk celery, sliced (about ½ cup)
½ cup uncooked medium egg noodles
1 can (5 ounces) SWANSON® Premium Chunk Chicken
   Breast or Chunk Chicken, drained

In medium saucepan mix broth, pepper, carrot and celery. Over medium-high heat, heat to a boil. Stir in noodles. Reduce heat to medium. Cook 10 minutes, stirring often. Add chicken and heat through.   *Serves 4*

*Top to bottom: Easy Vegetable Soup (page 70)
and Chicken Noodle Soup Express*

Easy Vegetable Soup

(photo on page 69)

Prep Time: 5 minutes   **Cook Time:** 25 minutes

2   cans (14½ ounces each) SWANSON® Chicken
    Broth (3½ cups)
3   cups CAMPBELL'S® Tomato Juice
1   teaspoon dried oregano leaves or Italian seasoning,
    crushed
½   teaspoon garlic powder or 4 cloves garlic, minced
¼   teaspoon pepper
1   bag (16 ounces) frozen vegetable combination
    (broccoli, cauliflower, carrots)
1   can (about 15 ounces) kidney beans or 1 can
    (about 16 ounces) white kidney (cannellini) beans,
    rinsed and drained

In large saucepan mix broth, tomato juice, oregano, garlic powder, pepper and vegetables. Over medium-high heat, heat to a boil. Cover and cook 10 minutes or until vegetables are tender. Add beans and heat through.   *Serves 8*

tip

For a change of taste, substitute 1 bag (16 ounces)
frozen Italian vegetable combination.

Mushroom Mozzarella Bruschetta

(photo on page 15)

Prep Time: 15 minutes   **Cook Time:** 5 minutes

1   loaf (about 1 pound) Italian bread (16-inches long), cut in half lengthwise
1   can (10¾ ounces) CAMPBELL'S® Condensed Cream of Mushroom Soup or 98% Fat Free Cream of Mushroom Soup
¼   teaspoon garlic powder
¼   teaspoon dried Italian seasoning, crushed
1   cup shredded mozzarella cheese (4 ounces)
1   tablespoon grated Parmesan cheese
1   small red pepper, chopped (about ½ cup)
2   green onions, chopped (about ¼ cup)

1. Bake bread on baking sheet at 400°F. for 5 minutes or until lightly toasted.

2. Mix soup, garlic powder and Italian seasoning. Stir in mozzarella cheese, Parmesan cheese, pepper and onions.

3. Spread soup mixture on bread. Bake 5 minutes or until cheese is melted. Cut each bread half into 4 pieces.   *Serves 8*

 **timesaver tip**

For convenience, use packaged pre-shredded mozzarella cheese. Half an 8-ounce package will provide the 1 cup needed for this recipe.

Chicken Broccoli Pockets

Prep Time: 15 minutes   **Cook Time:** 10 minutes

- 1 can (10¾ ounces) CAMPBELL'S® HEALTHY REQUEST Condensed Cream of Chicken Soup
- ¼ cup water
- 1 tablespoon lemon juice
- ¼ teaspoon garlic powder
- ⅛ teaspoon pepper
- 1 cup cooked broccoli flowerets
- 1 medium carrot, shredded (about ½ cup)
- 2 cups cubed cooked chicken
- 3 pita breads (6-inch), cut in half, forming 2 pockets

1. In medium saucepan mix soup, water, lemon juice, garlic powder, pepper, broccoli, carrot and chicken. Over medium heat, heat through.

2. Spoon ½ cup chicken mixture into each pita half.

Makes 6 sandwiches

Nutritional Values per Serving: Calories 202, Total Fat 4g, Saturated Fat 1g, Cholesterol 39mg, Sodium 404mg, Total Carbohydrate 24g, Protein 16g

Chicken Broccoli Potato Topper: Omit pita breads. Serve ¾ cup chicken mixture over each of 4 hot baked potatoes, split (about 2 pounds).

Serves 4

In this recipe, CAMPBELL'S® HEALTHY REQUEST provides a healthier, delicious alternative to a mayonnaise-based pocket sandwich filling.

Chicken Broccoli Pocket

Souper Sloppy Joes

Prep/Cook Time: 15 minutes

1 **pound ground beef**
1 **can (10¾ ounces) Campbell's® Condensed Tomato Soup**
¼ **cup water**
1 **tablespoon prepared yellow mustard**
6 **hamburger rolls, split**

1. Cook beef in medium skillet over medium-high heat until beef is browned, stirring to separate meat. Pour off fat.

2. Add soup, water and mustard. Heat through. Serve on rolls.

Serves 6

Buffalo-Style Burgers

Prep Time: 10 minutes   **Cook Time:** 20 minutes

1 **pound ground beef**
1 **can (10¾ ounces) Campbell's® Condensed Tomato Soup**
½ **teaspoon Louisiana-style hot sauce**
4 **hamburger rolls**
  Lettuce leaves, red onion slices, tomato slices (optional)
½ **cup crumbled blue cheese**

1. Shape beef into 4 patties, ½-inch thick.

2. Mix soup and hot sauce in saucepan. Heat to a boil. Cover and cook over low heat for 5 minutes; keep warm.

3. Grill or broil beef patties for 10 minutes or until done.

4. Serve burgers on rolls with lettuce, onion and tomato. Top with soup mixture. Sprinkle with cheese.

Serves 4

Buffalo-Style Burger

5-Minute Burrito Wraps

Prep/Cook Time: 5 minutes

- 1 can (11¼ ounces) CAMPBELL'S® Condensed Fiesta Chili Beef Soup
- 6 flour tortillas (8-inch)
  Shredded Cheddar cheese

1. Spoon 2 tablespoons soup down center of each tortilla. Top with cheese. Fold tortilla around filling.

2. Place seam-side down on microwave-safe plate and microwave on HIGH 2 minutes or until hot.

Makes 6 burritos

Souperburger Sandwiches

Prep Time: 5 minutes   **Cook Time:** 10 minutes

- 1 pound ground beef
- 1 medium onion, chopped (about ½ cup)
- 1 can (10¾ ounces) CAMPBELL'S® Condensed Cheddar Cheese Soup
- 1 tablespoon prepared mustard
- ⅛ teaspoon pepper
- 6 hamburger rolls, split and toasted

1. In medium skillet over medium-high heat, cook beef and onion until beef is browned, stirring to separate meat. Pour off fat.

2. Add soup, mustard and pepper. Reduce heat to low and heat through. Divide meat mixture among rolls.

Makes 6 sandwiches

5-Minute Burrito Wraps

Quick Beef 'n' Beans Tacos

Prep Time: 15 minutes   **Cook Time:** 10 minutes

- 1 **pound ground beef**
- 1 **small onion, chopped (about ¼ cup)**
- 1 **can (11¼ ounces) CAMPBELL'S® Condensed Fiesta Chili Beef Soup**
- ¼ **cup water**
- 10 **taco shells**
  Shredded Cheddar cheese, shredded lettuce, diced tomato and sour cream

1. In medium skillet over medium-high heat, cook beef and onion until beef is browned, stirring to separate meat. Pour off fat.

2. Add soup and water. Reduce heat to low. Cover and cook 5 minutes.

3. Divide meat mixture among taco shells. Top with cheese, lettuce, tomato and sour cream.   *Makes 10 tacos*

Easy Nachos

Prep/Cook Time: 15 minutes

- 1 **can (10¾ ounces) CAMPBELL'S® Condensed Cheddar Cheese Soup**
- ½ **cup PACE® Picante Sauce**
- 1 **bag (about 10 ounces) tortilla chips***
- 1 **medium tomato, chopped**
- ¼ **cup sliced pitted ripe olives**

1. Mix soup and picante sauce in saucepan. Heat through.

2. Serve over tortilla chips. Top with tomatoes and olives.   *Serves 6*

*To warm chips in microwave, place half on microwave-safe plate. Microwave on HIGH 1 minute. Repeat for remaining chips.

Quick Beef 'n' Beans Tacos

Cheesy Broccoli Potato Topper

Prep Time: 5 minutes   **Cook Time:** 5 minutes

> 1 can (10¾ ounces) CAMPBELL'S® Condensed Cheddar
>   Cheese Soup
> 4 large hot baked potatoes, split
> 1 cup cooked broccoli flowerets

1. Stir soup in can until soup is smooth.

2. Place hot baked potatoes on microwave-safe plate. Carefully fluff up potatoes with fork.

3. Top each potato with broccoli. Spoon soup over potatoes. Microwave on HIGH 4 minutes or until hot.   *Serves 4*

Baked Potatoes Olé

Prep Time: 5 minutes   **Cook Time:** 15 minutes

> 1 pound ground beef
> 1 tablespoon chili powder
> 1 cup PACE® Picante Sauce or Thick & Chunky Salsa
> 4 hot baked potatoes, split
>   Shredded Cheddar cheese

1. In medium skillet over medium-high heat, cook beef and chili powder until beef is browned, stirring to separate meat. Pour off fat.

2. Add picante sauce. Reduce heat to low and heat through. Serve over potatoes. Top with cheese.   *Serves 4*

Clockwise from top: Cheesy Picante Potatoes (page 86), Baked Potato Olé and Cheesy Broccoli Potato Topper

QUICK SIDE DISHES

One-Dish Pasta & Vegetables

Prep Time: 15 minutes   **Cook Time:** 15 minutes

1½ cups uncooked corkscrew macaroni
 2 medium carrots, sliced (about 1 cup)
 1 cup broccoli flowerets
 1 can (10¾ ounces) CAMPBELL'S® Condensed Cheddar
    Cheese Soup
 ½ cup milk
 1 tablespoon prepared mustard

1. In large saucepan prepare macaroni according to package directions. Add carrots and broccoli for last 5 minutes of cooking time. Drain.

2. In same pan mix soup, milk, mustard and macaroni mixture. Over medium heat, heat through, stirring often.   *Serves 5*

One-Dish Pasta & Vegetables

Cheese Fries

Prep/Cook Time: 20 minutes

1 bag (32 ounces) frozen French fried potatoes
1 can (10¾ ounces) CAMPBELL'S® Condensed
   Cheddar Cheese Soup

1. Bake potatoes according to package directions.

2. Push potatoes into center of baking sheet. Stir soup in can
and spoon over potatoes.

3. Bake 3 minutes or until soup is hot.

Serves 6

Saucy Asparagus

Prep Time: 10 minutes   **Cook Time:** 15 minutes

1 can (10¾ ounces) CAMPBELL'S® Condensed Cream
   of Asparagus Soup
2 tablespoons milk
1½ pounds asparagus, trimmed, cut into 1-inch pieces
   (about 3 cups) or 2 packages (10 ounces each)
   frozen asparagus cuts

1. In medium saucepan mix soup and milk. Over medium heat, heat
to a boil, stirring occasionally.

2. Add asparagus. Reduce heat to low. Cover and cook 10 minutes
or until asparagus is tender, stirring occasionally.

Serves 6

Saucy Asparagus

Nacho Potato Topper

Prep/Cook Time: 10 minutes

1 can (10¾ ounces) CAMPBELL'S® Condensed
    Cheddar Cheese Soup
½ cup PACE® Chunky Salsa
4 large hot baked potatoes, split*
    Sour cream for garnish

1. Mix soup and salsa in saucepan. Heat through.

2. Serve over potatoes. Top with sour cream.   *Serves 4*

**To bake potatoes, pierce potatoes with fork. Bake at 400° F. for
1 hour or microwave on HIGH 10 1/2 minutes or until fork-tender.*

Cheesy Picante Potatoes

(photo on page 81)

Prep Time: 10 minutes   **Cook Time:** 10 minutes

1 can (10¾ ounces) CAMPBELL'S® Condensed Cheddar
    Cheese Soup
½ cup PACE® Picante Sauce or Thick & Chunky Salsa
1 teaspoon garlic powder
4 cups cubed cooked potatoes (about 4 medium)
    Paprika
2 tablespoons chopped fresh cilantro

In medium skillet mix soup, picante sauce and garlic powder. Add
potatoes. Over medium heat, heat through, stirring often. Sprinkle
with paprika and cilantro. Serve with additional picante sauce.

Serves 6 to 8

Garlic Mashed Potatoes

(photo on page 23)

Prep Time: 10 minutes   **Cook Time:** 15 minutes

2 cans (14½ ounces each) SWANSON®
   Seasoned Chicken Broth with Roasted Garlic
5 large potatoes, cut into 1-inch pieces

1. In medium saucepan place broth and potatoes. Over high heat, heat to a boil. Reduce heat to medium. Cover and cook 10 minutes or until potatoes are tender. Drain, reserving broth.

2. Mash potatoes with *1¼ cups* reserved broth. If needed, add additional broth until potatoes are desired consistency.

Serves about 6

tip

Skinny Mashed Potatoes: Substitute 2 cans (14½ ounces *each*) SWANSON® Chicken Broth for Chicken Broth with Roasted Garlic.

Vegetable-Rice Pilaf

(photo on page 59)

Prep Time: 5 minutes   **Cook Time:** 20 minutes

Vegetable cooking spray
¼ cup chopped green or red pepper
2 cloves garlic, minced
½ teaspoon dried basil leaves, crushed
⅛ teaspoon black pepper
1 cup uncooked regular long-grain white rice
1 can (14 ounces) SWANSON® Chicken Broth (1½ cups)
¾ cup frozen mixed vegetables

1. Spray medium skillet with cooking spray and heat over medium heat 1 minute. Add green pepper, garlic, basil, black pepper and rice. Cook until rice is browned and green pepper is tender-crisp, stirring constantly.

2. Stir in broth. Heat to a boil. Reduce heat to low. Cover and cook 10 minutes.

3. Stir in vegetables. Cover and cook 10 minutes more or until rice is done and most of liquid is absorbed.   *Serves 4*

Try this delicious side dish as a healthier alternative to high-sodium packaged rice dishes.

Fiesta Rice

(photo on front cover)

Prep Time: 5 minutes   **Cook/Stand Time:** 10 minutes

> 1   **can (10½ ounces) CAMPBELL'S® Condensed Chicken Broth**
> ½   **cup water**
> ½   **cup PACE Thick & Chunky Salsa**
> 2   **cups uncooked instant white rice**

1. In medium saucepan mix broth, water and salsa. Over medium-high heat, heat to a boil.

2. Stir in rice. Cover and remove from heat. Let stand 5 minutes. Fluff with fork.   *Serves 4*

Quick Lemon-Broccoli Rice

(photo on page 37)

Prep Time: 10 minutes   **Cook Time:** 15 minutes

> 1   **can (10½ ounces) CAMPBELL'S® Condensed Chicken Broth**
> 1   **cup small broccoli flowerets**
> 1   **small carrot, shredded (about ⅓ cup)**
> 1¼   **cups uncooked instant white rice**
> 2   **teaspoons lemon juice**
>   **Generous dash pepper**

1. In medium saucepan over high heat, heat broth to a boil. Add broccoli and carrot. Reduce heat to low. Cover and cook 5 minutes or until vegetables are tender.

2. Stir in rice, lemon juice and pepper. Cover and remove from heat. Let stand 5 minutes. Fluff with fork.   *Serves 4*

Heavenly Sweet Potatoes

Prep Time: 10 minutes   **Bake Time:** 20 minutes

Vegetable cooking spray
1 can (40 ounces) cut sweet potatoes in heavy syrup, drained
¼ teaspoon ground cinnamon
⅛ teaspoon ground ginger
¾ cup SWANSON® Chicken Broth
2 cups miniature marshmallows

1. Spray 1½-quart casserole with cooking spray.

2. Place potatoes, cinnamon and ginger in mixer bowl. Beat until potatoes are fluffy and almost smooth, using mixer at medium speed. Add broth and beat until well blended. Spoon potato mixture in prepared dish. Top with marshmallows.

3. Bake at 350°F. for 20 minutes or until heated through and marshmallows are golden brown.   *Serves 8*

Creamy Vegetables in Pastry Shells

(photo on page 67)

Bake Time: 30 minutes*   **Prep/Cook Time:** 15 minutes

1   package (10 ounces) PEPPERIDGE FARM®
     Frozen Puff Pastry Shells
1   can (10¾ ounces) CAMPBELL'S® Condensed
     Cream of Mushroom Soup or 98% Fat Free
     Cream of Mushroom Soup
⅓   cup milk or water
1   bag (16 ounces) frozen vegetable combination
     (broccoli, cauliflower, carrots), cooked and drained

1. Prepare pastry shells according to package directions.

2. In medium saucepan mix soup and milk. Over medium heat, heat through, stirring often. Divide vegetables among pastry shells. Spoon sauce over vegetables and pastry shells.

Serves 6

Bake pastry shells while preparing sauce mixture.

tip

Substitute 2 cups broccoli flowerets,
1 cup cauliflowerets and 2 medium carrots,
sliced (about 2 cups), cooked and drained,
for the frozen vegetable combination.

Recipe Index

METRIC CONVERSION CHART

VOLUME MEASUREMENTS (dry)

1/8 teaspoon = 0.5 mL
1/4 teaspoon = 1 mL
1/2 teaspoon = 2 mL
3/4 teaspoon = 4 mL
1 teaspoon = 5 mL
1 tablespoon = 15 mL
2 tablespoons = 30 mL
1/4 cup = 60 mL
1/3 cup = 75 mL
1/2 cup = 125 mL
2/3 cup = 150 mL
3/4 cup = 175 mL
1 cup = 250 mL
2 cups = 1 pint = 500 mL
3 cups = 750 mL
4 cups = 1 quart = 1 L

VOLUME MEASUREMENTS (fluid)

1 fluid ounce (2 tablespoons) = 30 mL
4 fluid ounces (1/2 cup) = 125 mL
8 fluid ounces (1 cup) = 250 mL
12 fluid ounces (1 1/2 cups) = 375 mL
16 fluid ounces (2 cups) = 500 mL

WEIGHTS (mass)

1/2 ounce = 15 g
1 ounce = 30 g
3 ounces = 90 g
4 ounces = 120 g
8 ounces = 225 g
10 ounces = 285 g
12 ounces = 360 g
16 ounces = 1 pound = 450 g

DIMENSIONS

1/16 inch = 2 mm
1/8 inch = 3 mm
1/4 inch = 6 mm
1/2 inch = 1.5 cm
3/4 inch = 2 cm
1 inch = 2.5 cm

OVEN TEMPERATURES

250°F = 120°C
275°F = 140°C
300°F = 150°C
325°F = 160°C
350°F = 180°C
375°F = 190°C
400°F = 200°C
425°F = 220°C
450°F = 230°C

BAKING PAN SIZES

Utensil	Size in Inches/Quarts	Metric Volume	Size in Centimeters
Baking or	8×8×2	2 L	20×20×5
Cake Pan	9×9×2	2.5 L	23×23×5
(square or	12×8×2	3 L	30×20×5
rectangular)	13×9×2	3.5 L	33×23×5
Loaf Pan	8×4×3	1.5 L	20×10×7
	9×5×3	2 L	23×13×7
Round Layer	8×1½	1.2 L	20×4
Cake Pan	9×1½	1.5 L	23×4
Pie Plate	8×1¼	750 mL	20×3
	9×1¼	1 L	23×3
Baking Dish	1 quart	1 L	—
or Casserole	1½ quart	1.5 L	—
	2 quart	2 L	—